Abi Cushman

FLAMINGOS ARE PRETTY FUNKY

A [not so] serious guide

GREENWILLOW BOOKS
An Imprint of HarperCollinsPublishers

Look closely.
You just might be able to spot—

Oh, wait. Stop. You're *too* close.
Back up a little.

A little more . . .

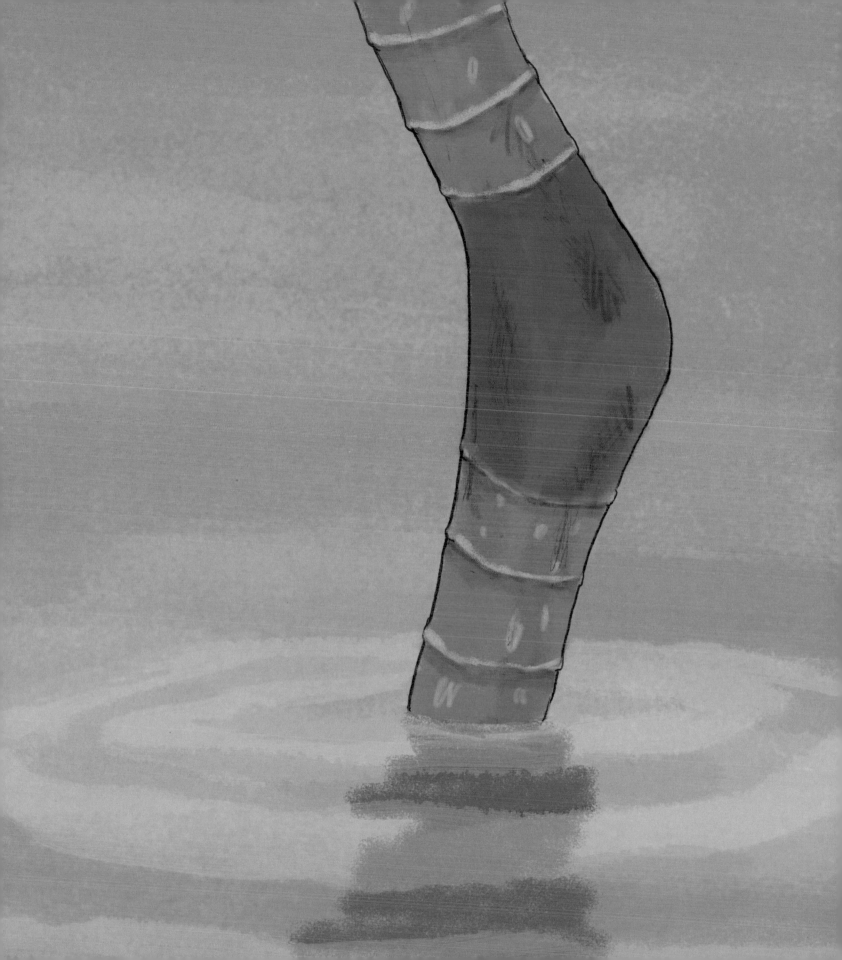

There!

Behold the flamingo, a tall wading bird known for its bright-pink color.

Hellooooo!

Oh . . . and uh,
also that snake over there.
Behind the rock.
Known for its . . .
drab pea-greeny color.

I actually consider it
more of an olive tone.

Flamingos live on every continent except Australia and Antarctica.

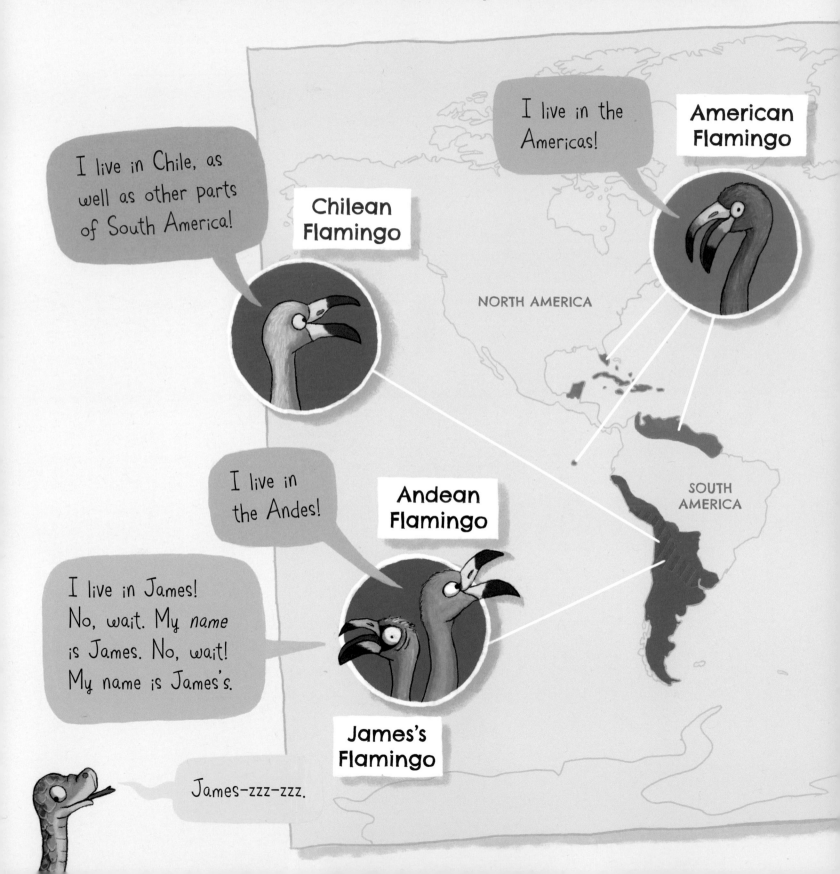

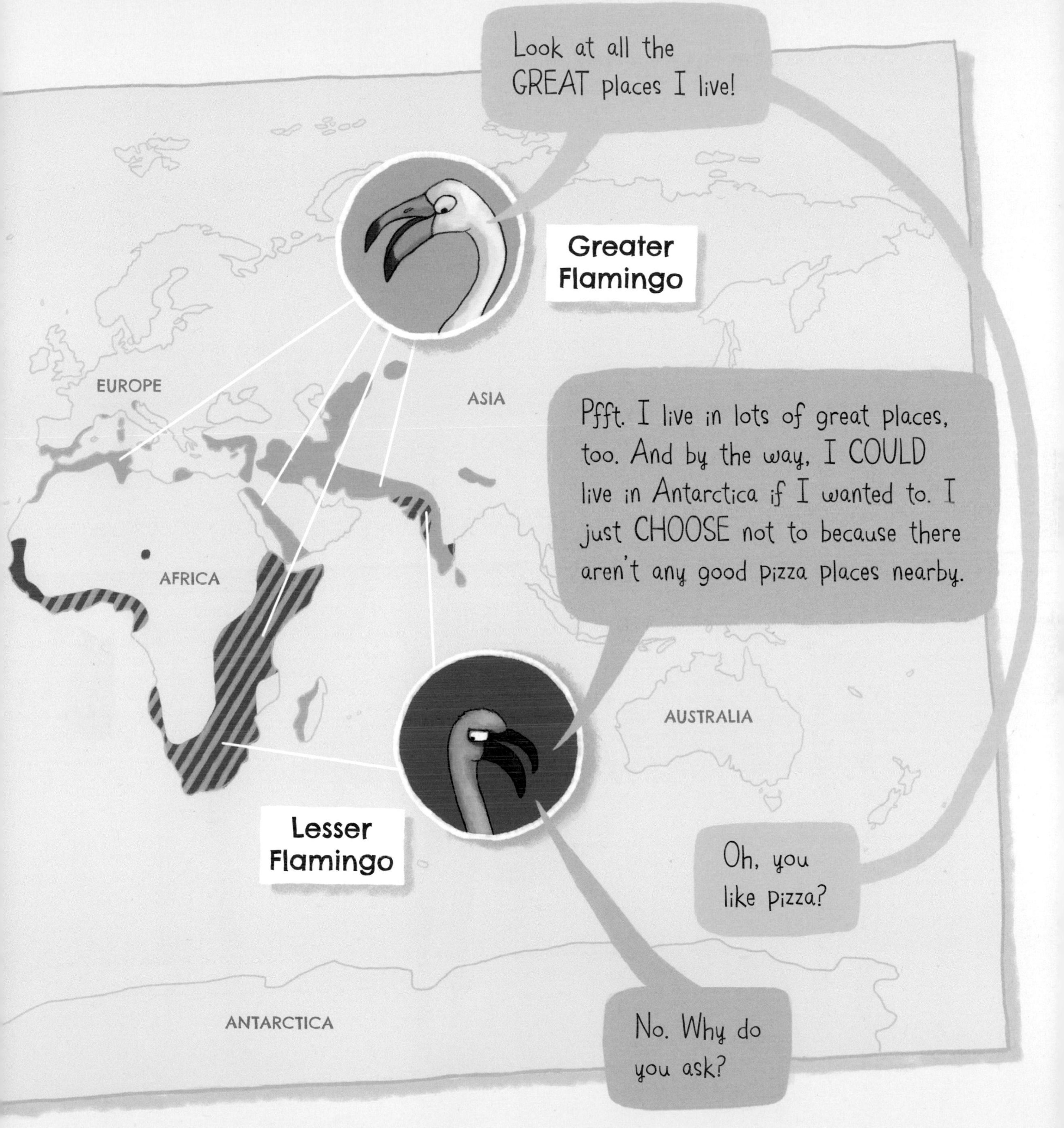
Look at all the GREAT places I live!
Greater Flamingo
EUROPE
ASIA
AFRICA
Pfft. I live in lots of great places, too. And by the way, I COULD live in Antarctica if I wanted to. I just CHOOSE not to because there aren't any good pizza places nearby.
AUSTRALIA
Lesser Flamingo
Oh, you like pizza?
ANTARCTICA
No. Why do you ask?

There are six species of flamingos:

Flamingos get their pink color by eating it. The algae and shrimp they feed on contain orange and red pigments called carotenoids. These chemicals are then absorbed into the flamingos' feathers, beak, and legs, and give them that vibrant pink hue.

Colorful Cuisine

Carotenoids are organic pigments made by plants and algae. They give vegetables like carrots and pumpkins their orange color.

Other animals besides flamingos get their color from their food. Shrimp turn orange after feeding on the same algae that flamingos eat. Cardinals intensify their crimson hues by eating colorful berries.

NOTE: Although carotenoid-rich algae can be red, it is often green, blue, or brown. This is because it contains other colorful chemicals in addition to carotenoids.

During the breeding season, flamingos brighten their pink coloring with natural makeup. A gland near their tail produces a reddish-orange oil, which they rub directly onto their cheeks and then apply to their other feathers. Once flamingos find a partner, they cut back on their makeup usage significantly.

Hey, check out my new makeup. It's from a place called the uropygial gland.

Oh, I love that place! That's where I get my makeup, too. And it's so conveniently located right there on my tail.

Makeup is great for enhancing your natural beauty, don't you think?

?!

Flamingos are fantastic dancers. To attract a mate, a group of flamingos performs a courtship dance, which includes moves like stretching their heads high in the air and waving them around, lifting their wings, marching in unison, and honking.

Flamingo nests look like tiny volcanoes. Both the male and female flamingo work together to form a mud mound about twelve inches tall. Then the female lays one large white egg at the top of the mound.

Flamin-GROW

Flamingo chicks are born with fluffy gray feathers and straight beaks. Once their beaks start to curve (at around four weeks), they can scoop up food from the water on their own. After two to three years, their adult feathers grow in and start turning pink.

Both flamingo parents produce a bright-red liquid in their throats called crop milk, which they regurgitate directly into their chick's mouth. The carotenoids that would normally go into the parents' feathers go into the crop milk instead, leaving their plumage pale pink or even white at the end of the breeding season.

Are you okay? You look a little pale.

ME? I feel great! Never been better, in fact!

Now, who wants more milk from my throat?

MEEEEE!

Although flamingos are good swimmers, they spend most of their time wading in shallow lakes and lagoons.

Some flamingos wade in water that is really salty, near boiling hot, or filled with corrosive chemicals. Corrosive chemicals will burn your skin and eyes if you touch them.

And some flamingos wade in lakes high in the mountains where it's cold.

So cold that the water sometimes freezes around the flamingos' legs at night. But luckily for flamingos . . .

. . . they have tough scales on top of the thick, leathery skin on their legs and feet. This protects them from toxic water and extreme temperatures.

Wow! Check you out! That is impressive!

Ah, yes! I stretch five times a day.

No, I mean, your leg is *exceptionally* leathery and scaly! What's your skin-care routine?

OH . . . thank you! My secret is never using lotion and just, you know, being a flamingo.

Their ability to live in such harsh environments means flamingos don't have to worry about lots of other animals inhabiting the same area and eating all their food. Or worse, eating *them*.

Can you believe no one else has moved into this lake? Beautiful view, toxic water, all the algae you can eat . . . what more could you ask for?

Yes, thank you for recommending this rock! I have such a beautiful view of those hungry jackals on the shore. I don't think I'll ever leave!

We can get pizza delivered out here, right?

Flamingos always eat with their heads upside down. They slurp up muddy water, then strain food like algae, shrimp, insect larvae, and mollusks from it with their special curved beaks.

Upside-down eating is the only way to go if you really want to get that intense mud flavor.

You're so right! I can totally taste the mud on this pizza now.

Unique Beaks

Flamingo beaks are specially adapted for feeding upside down and for filtering food from the water. Here's how:

Tongue Pump

Flamingos use their thick tongues to rapidly pump water in and out of their beaks. Curved spines on the back of the tongue help push food to the throat.

Beak Comb

Flamingo beaks contain comb-like structures called lamellae, which trap food inside and let water flow through.

Salt Sifter

Flamingos can drink salt water because they have glands in their heads that filter the salt out through their nostrils.

Movable Upper Bill

Unlike other birds (and people), a flamingo's upper jaw is not fixed to its skull and can move up and down. This, along with the curved shape of the bill, helps them scoop up water while their head is upside down.

Wow! You really know how to turn that frown upside down!

Flamingos often stand, and even sleep, on one leg. On one leg, their weight is perfectly balanced, and the joints in that leg lock in place. Since they don't have to use their muscles to keep their balance, it actually takes less effort for a flamingo to stand on one leg than on two.

Wow! You are really good at balancing on two legs. I have to use just one leg or else I fall down.

Keep trying, and you'll get it eventually!

The joint midway up a flamingo's leg is an ankle, not a knee. Flamingo knees are located inside their bodies and bend just like human knees do.

Bet you thought my knee was bending backward, but it's really my ankle!

What's a knee?

Inside Look

Normally, a flamingo's knees are hidden by its feathers and flesh. Let's look inside to see the leg bone structure.

See my knee? Hey, that rhymed!

knee

tibiotarsus

femur

ankle

tarsometatarsus

Flamingos are very social and live in large groups called colonies or flamboyances. Living in a colony helps protect them from predators such as jackals, eagles, storks, and vultures, who prey on flamingos or their eggs.

But while thousands may live together in a colony, flamingos tend to form close bonds with just a few members of the group.

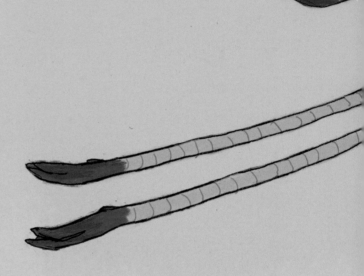

Who's ready to fla-MINGLE? I brought algae snacks!

Hello? Anyone?

Hello . . . James-zzz-zzz?

Flamingos can fly as fast as 55 mph (though they typically go about 35 mph). They can fly as high as 19,000 feet and can cover long distances without stopping. In fact, one flamingo was tracked flying 700 miles in a single trip!

Some flamingos migrate on a seasonal basis, while others travel to find better nesting grounds or more food as needed. And some flamingos just stay put!

But even if flamingos do take off for a little bit,

they usually come back, to stand around in toxic water, slurping up mud with their friends.

And that makes these color-eating, one-leg-sleeping birds pretty funky. Pretty funky and pretty fabulous.

Greater Flamingo

Scientific Name: *Phoenicopterus roseus*

Height: 47–59 inches

Weight: 4.5–9 pounds

Conservation Status: Least Concern

Threats: Low water levels; pollution from agricultural runoff

Greater Flamingo

Still haven't come up with a jazzier name, I see . . .

Lesser Flamingo

Scientific Name: *Phoeniconaias minor*

Height: 31–36 inches

Weight: 3.5–4.5 pounds

Conservation Status: Near Threatened

Threats: Habitat loss due to pollution and development

Lesser Flamingo

American, or Caribbean, Flamingo

American, or Caribbean, Flamingo

Scientific Name: *Phoenicopterus ruber*

Height: 47–57 inches

Weight: 4-8 pounds

Conservation Status: Least Concern

Threats: Pollution from agricultural runoff

Chilean Flamingo

Chilean Flamingo
Scientific Name: *Phoenicopterus chilensis*
Height: 41–51 inches
Weight: 5.5-7.5 pounds
Conservation Status: Near Threatened
Threats: Egg harvesting; habitat loss due to mining and water management

Andean Flamingo

Andean Flamingo
Scientific Name: *Phoenicoparrus andinus*
Height: 39–55 inches
Weight: 3.5–9 pounds
Conservation Status: Vulnerable
Threats: Egg harvesting; low water levels; habitat loss due to mining and water management

James's, or Puna, Flamingo

James's, or Puna, Flamingo
Scientific Name: *Phoenicoparrus jamesi*
Height: 30–36 inches
Height: 3.5–6.5 pounds
Conservation Status: Near Threatened
Threats: Egg harvesting; habitat loss due to mining and water management

James-zzz-zzz-zzz-zzz-zzz-zzz!

Glossary

Andes: A mountain range located on the western side of South America.

Carotenoid [cuh-RAH-tuh-noid]: An organic orange or red pigment made by plants and algae.

Colony: A group of flamingos.

Corrosive: Having the capability to burn or eat away a substance by chemical reaction.

Crop milk: A bright-red liquid that flamingos produce in their throats to feed their young.

Flamboyance: Another name for a group of flamingos.

Knee: The joint that connects your thigh bone to your shin bone.

Lamellae [luh-MEL-ee]: Comblike structures in a flamingo's beak.

Pigment: A natural coloring substance found in animals or plants.

Regurgitate [ree-GUR-juh-tayt]: To bring up swallowed food or other substances from the digestive tract back to the mouth.

Tarsometatarsus [tar-so-meh-tuh-TAR-sus]: The lower leg bone on a bird.

Tibiotarsus [tib-ee-oh-TAR-suhs]: The bone between the knee and ankle on a bird.

Uropygial [yur-uh-PIJ-ee-uhl] **gland:** An organ found at the base of a bird's tail feathers that secretes oil.

Ohhh! That's what a knee is!

Excuse me? No, I'm not. YOU'RE a pij-ee-uhl gland!

Further Reading

Amat, J.A., Rendón, M.A., Garrido-Fernández, J. et al. "Greater flamingos *Phoenicopterus roseus* use uropygial secretions as makeup." *Behav Ecol Sociobiol* 65, 665–673 (2011). www.doi.org/10.1007/s00265-010-1068-z

Anderson, Justin, producer. *Planet Earth II*. Season 1, episode 2, "Mountains." Aired November 13, 2016 on BBC One.

Arthur, Amy. "Flamingos Make Long-Lasting Friendships, Same-Sex Bonds and 'Married' Couplings." *BBC Science Focus*, April 16, 2020.
https://www.sciencefocus.com/nature/flamingos-make-long-lasting-friendships-same-sex-bonds-and-married-couplings/

Chang, Young-Hui and Lena H. Ting. 2017. "Mechanical evidence that flamingos can support their body on one leg with little active muscular force." *Biology Letters* 13: 20160948.20160948
www.doi.org/10.1098/rsbl.2016.0948

Dzombak, Rebecca. "Flamingos Dye Their Sun-Faded Feathers to Stay Pretty in Pink." *ScienceNews*, October 26, 2021.
www.sciencenews.org/article/flamingo-feathers-dye-pink-biology

Ehrlich, Paul, David S. Dobkin, Darryl Wheye. *The Birder's Handbook: A Field Guide to the Natural History of North American Birds*. New York: Touchstone, 1988.

Elder, Scott. "Pink Power: 5 Ways Flamingos are the Most Extreme Birds on Earth." *National Geographic Kids*, February, 2022.

Kennedy, Merrit. "Scientists Pinpoint How a Flamingo Balances on One Leg." National Public Radio, May 25, 2017.
www.npr.org/sections/thetwo-way/2017/05/25/530046238/scientists-pinpoint-how-a-flamingo-balances-on-one-leg

Rose, Paul. "Africa's Most Toxic Lakes are a Paradise for Fearless Flamingos." *The Conversation*, January 5, 2017.
www.theconversation.com/africas-most-toxic-lakes-are-a-paradise-for-fearless-flamingos-70817

Salvador, A., M. Á. Rendón, J. A. Amat, and M. Rendón-Martos (2022). "Greater Flamingo (*Phoenicopterus roseus*), version 2.0." In *Birds of the World* (S. M. Billerman, Editor). Cornell Lab of Ornithology, Ithaca, New York.
https://birdsoftheworld.org/bow/species/grefla3/2.0/introduction

"Underwater Flamingo Feeding." San Diego Zoo, June 23, 2020. www.youtube.com/watch?v=-1BF2XqboOo

To Jammie, who loves flamingos

Flamingos Are Pretty Funky: A (Not So) Serious Guide. Copyright © 2024 by Abi Cushman. All rights reserved. Manufactured in Italy. For information address HarperCollins Children's Books, a division of HarperCollins Publishers, 195 Broadway, New York, NY 10007. www.harpercollinschildrens.com. The full-color art was drawn in pencil and colored digitally. The text type is 16-point TT Norms Pro. Library of Congress Cataloging-in-Publication Data: Names: Cushman, Abi, author. Title: Flamingos are pretty funky : a (not so) serious guide / Abi Cushman. Description: First edition. | New York, NY : Greenwillow Books, an imprint of HarperCollins Publishers, [2024] | Includes bibliographical references. | Audience: Ages 4–8 | Summary: "An introduction to the amazing and unusual world of flamingos and their habitats"—Provided by publisher. Identifiers: LCCN 2023053855 | ISBN 9780063234444 (hardcover) Subjects: LCSH: Flamingos—Juvenile literature. | Flamingos—Juvenile humor. | Flamingos—Behavior—Juvenile literature. Classification: LCC QL696.C56 C87 2024 | DDC 598.3/5—dc23/eng/20231221 LC record available at https://lccn.loc.gov/2023053855   24 25 26 27 28 RTLO 10 9 8 7 6 5 4 3 2 1 First Edition

 Greenwillow Books